ABC's FROM JESUS

By Shy Meeks

Copyright © 2013 by Shy Meeks

ABC'S FROM JESUS
by Shy Meeks

Printed in the United States of America

ISBN 9781628398762

All rights reserved solely by the author. The author guarantees all contents are original and do not infringe upon the legal rights of any other person or work. No part of this book may be reproduced in any form without the permission of the author. The views expressed in this book are not necessarily those of the publisher.

www.xulonpress.com

"I Can Do All Things Through Christ Who Strengthens Me."

Philippians 4:13

is for Adam

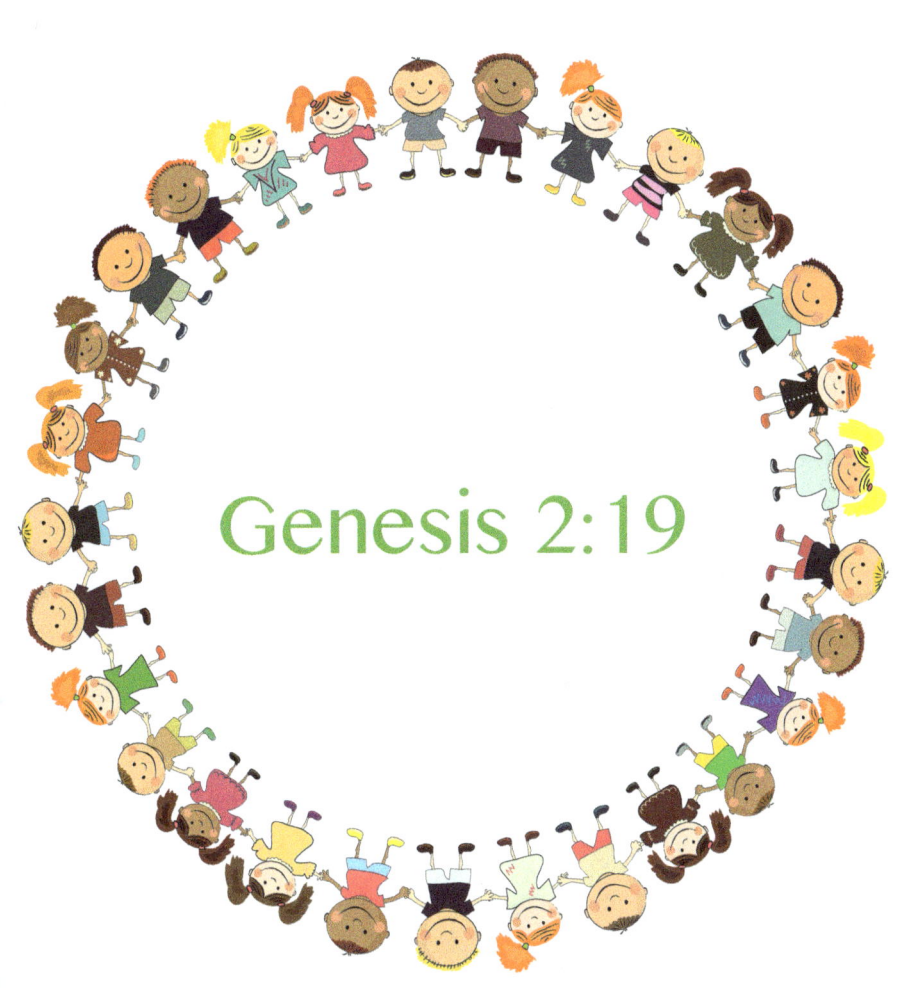

is for Bishop

is for Christ

is for David

is for Eve

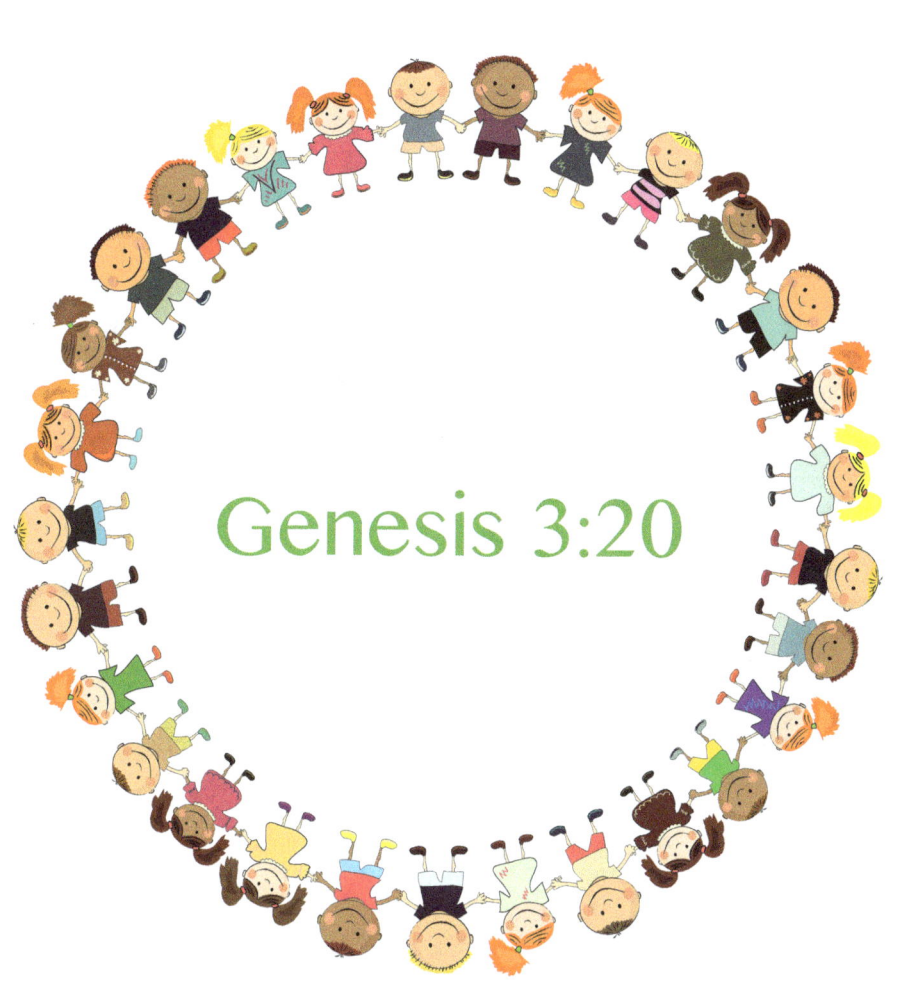

is for Faith

is for God

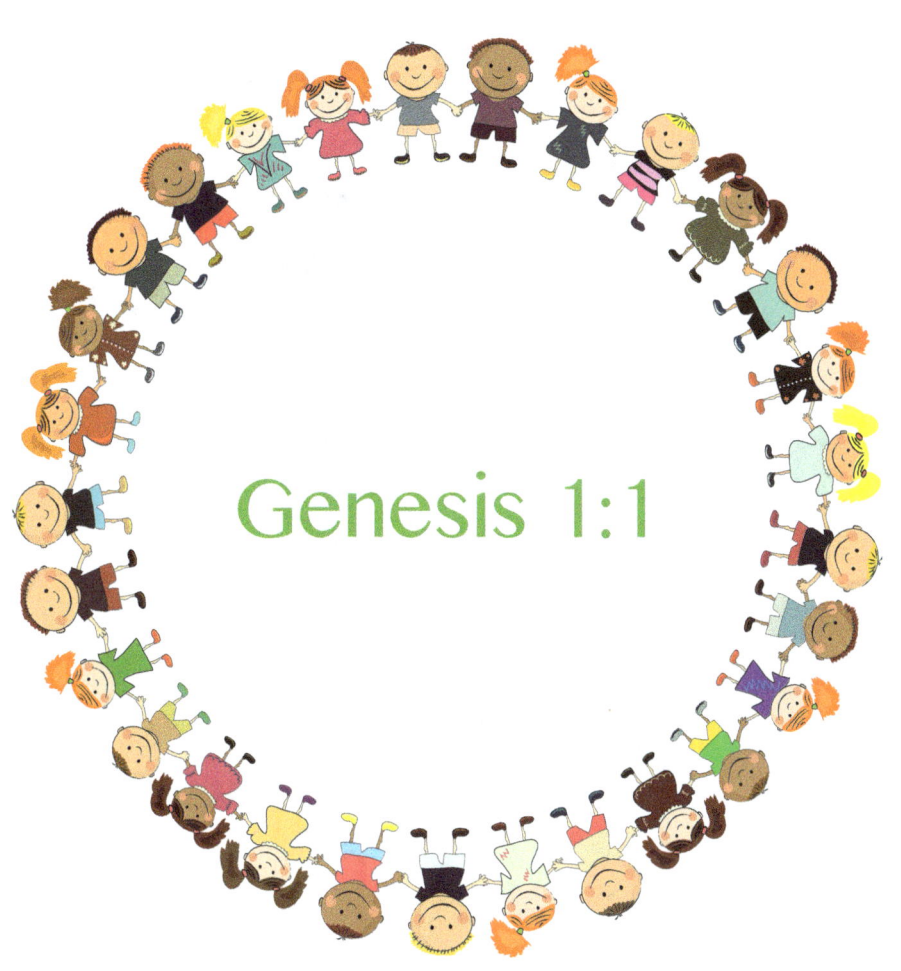

is for Honor

is for Isaac

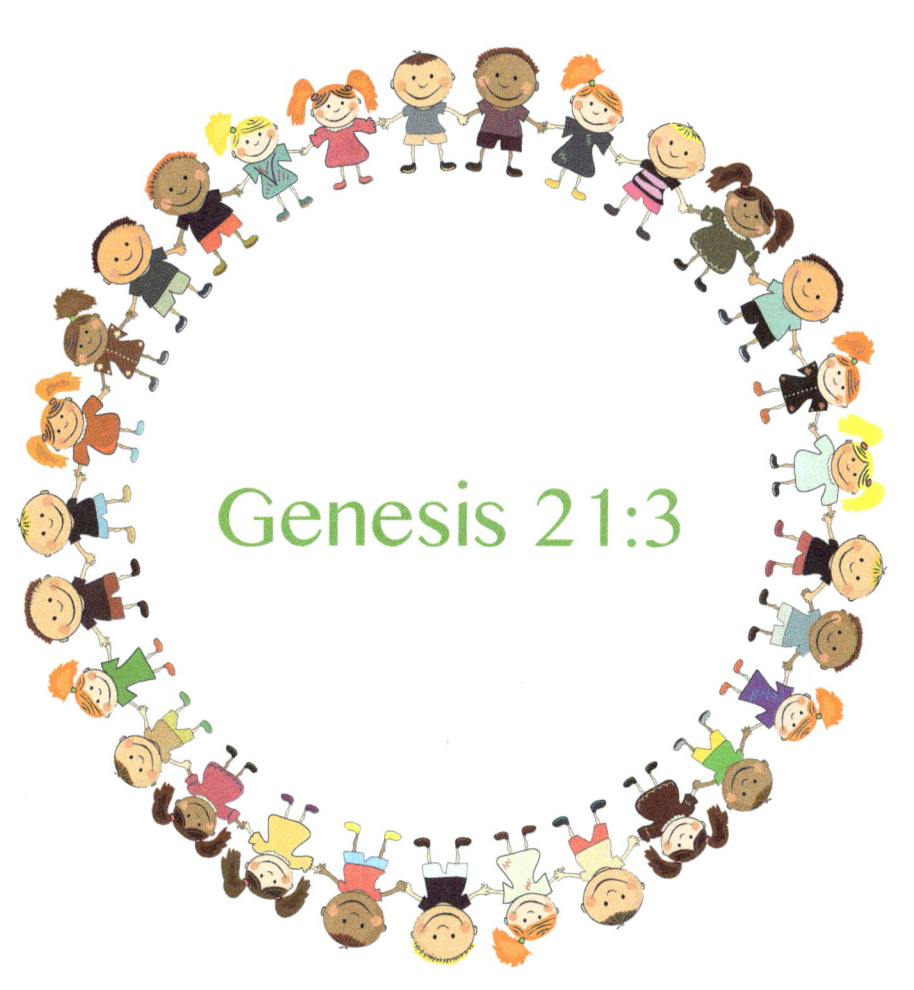

is for Jesus

is for Keeper

is for Love

is for Mordecai

is for Naomi

is for Omega

is for Prayer

is for Quench

is for Receive

is for Savior

is for Twelve

Luke 6:12-13

is for Unity

is for Virtue

is for Wisdom

is for Xerxes

is for Young

is for Zion

www.ingramcontent.com/pod-product-compliance
Lightning Source LLC
LaVergne TN
LVHW022001060526
838201LV00048B/1651